T0009835

RECHARGE

RECHARGE

Meditations
& Inspirations

MANDALA

SAN RAFAEL · LOS ANGELES · LONDON

Meditation directly impacts our nervous system by reducing the body's production of stress-related chemicals, such as cortisol. It's a great way to recharge our personal battery.

—LAURIE BUCHANAN

A CHANGE IS AS GOOD AS A REST.

—STEPHEN KING

An early morning
walk is a blessing
for the whole day.

—HENRY DAVID
THOREAU

Your sacred space
is where you can
find yourself over
and over again.

—JOSEPH CAMPBELL

Everything in
nature invites us
constantly to be
what we are.

—GRETEL EHRLICH

"What is the
scent of water?"

"Renewal.
The goodness
of God coming
down like dew."

—ELIZABETH GOUDGE

Don't underestimate the value of doing nothing, of just going along, listening to all the things you can't hear, and not bothering.

—A. A. MILNE

Nature's peace will flow into you as sunshine flows into trees. The winds will blow their own freshness into you, and the storms their energy.

—JOHN MUIR

ISN'T IT NICE
TO THINK THAT
TOMORROW
IS A NEW
DAY WITH
NO MISTAKES
IN IT YET?

—L. M. MONTGOMERY

If we surrendered
to earth's intelligence
we could rise up
rooted, like trees.

—RAINER MARIA RILKE

Everybody needs beauty as well as bread, places to play in and pray in, where nature may heal and give strength to body and soul.

—JOHN MUIR

Remember, you are spiritually recharged during sleep, and adequate sleep is essential to produce joy and vitality in life.

—JOSEPH MURPHY

THERE IS VIRTUE
IN WORK,
AND THERE IS
VIRTUE IN REST.
USE BOTH AND
OVERLOOK
NEITHER.

—ALAN COHEN

What lies behind us
and what lies before
us are tiny matters
compared to what
lies within us.

—UNKNOWN

Be patient with yourself. Self-growth is tender; it's holy ground. There's no greater investment.

—STEPHEN COVEY

I think it's important
to try to be present
with whatever it
is you're doing.
And if you can't
be present,
take a break.

—EMILY GIFFIN

Looking after my
health today gives
me a better hope
for tomorrow.

—ANNE SHCAEF

Gracious words
are refreshing
to the soul.

—LAILAH GIFTY AKITA

IF YOU WANT
TO CONQUER
THE ANXIETY OF
LIFE, LIVE IN THE
MOMENT, LIVE
IN THE BREATH.

—AMIT RAY

When we are depleted, our giving is empty. Today I take a moment to recharge, fill up with love for my life and all of its character so that I may give from a place of overflowing.

—LISA WIMBERGER

You must learn to let go. Release the stress. You were never in control anyway.

—STEVEN MARABOLI

WHAT LOVE
LAYS BARE
IN ME IS
ENERGY.

—ROLAND BARTHES

Stop, breathe,
look around
and embrace the
miracle of each day,
the miracle of life.

—JEFFREY A. WHITE

When you connect to the silence within you, that is when you can make sense of the disturbance going on around you.

—STEPHEN RICHARDS

THINGS
ARE
ALWAYS
BETTER
IN THE
MORNING.

—HARPER LEE

There is something
infinitely healing
in the repeated
refrains of nature.

—RACHEL CARSON

Rest when you're tired. Take a break when life stales. Take time to recharge your battery. Energy isn't something you have—it's something you are.

—MELODY BEATTIE

Certainly, work is
not always required
of a man. There
is such a thing as
a sacred idleness,
the cultivation
of which is now
fearfully neglected.

—GEORGE MACDONALD

REST AND BE THANKFUL.

—WILLIAM WORDSWORTH

If you neglect to recharge a battery, it dies. And if you run full speed ahead without stopping for water, you lose momentum to finish the race.

—OPRAH WINFREY

One day a week
I seek to rest
from earthly toil
and sorrow.
Revitalized,
I find the strength
to battle new
tomorrows.

—RICHELLE E.
GOODRICH

Just because you
take breaks doesn't
mean you're broken.

—CURTIS TYRONE JONES

Your true passion for life is hidden away within you. Your inner child holds the key to this. Take time for yourself, recharge, and let your inner child come out to play every once in a while.

—CHRISTINE E. SZYMANSKI

The mind can
go in a thousand
directions, but on
this beautiful path,
I walk in peace.
With each step,
the wind blows.
With each step,
a flower blooms.

—THICH NHAT HAHN

Slowing down does not indicate that you are giving up. It simply means that your soul is seeking some well-earned recharge.

—CHRISTINE E. SZYMANSKI

Restore your attention or bring it to a new level by dramatically slowing down whatever you're doing.

—SHARON SALZBERG

Success comes from the inside out. In order to change what is on the outside, you must first change what is on the inside.

—IDOWU KOYENIKAN

Breath is the finest
gift of nature.
Be grateful for this
wonderful gift.

—AMIT RAY

HAVE PATIENCE WITH ALL THINGS. BUT FIRST OF ALL WITH YOURSELF.

—FRANCIS DE SALES

Taking time to rest, renew, and refresh yourself isn't wasted time. Recharge. Choose what energizes you.

—MELODY BEATTIE

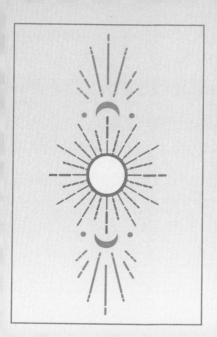

It's a good idea
always to do
something relaxing
prior to making an
important decision
in your life.

—PAULO COELHO

You find peace
not by rearranging
the circumstances
of your life but
by realizing who
you are at the
deepest level.

—ECKHART TOLLE

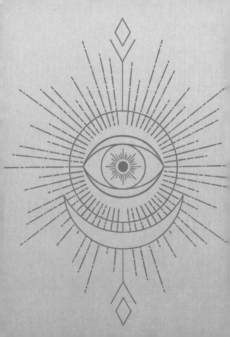

To lie sometimes
on the grass under
trees on a summer's
day, listening
to the murmur
of the water, is
by no means a
waste of time.

—JOHN LUBBOCK

SOLITUDE
IS WHERE I
PLACE MY
CHAOS TO
REST AND
AWAKEN
MY INNER
PEACE.

—NIKKI ROWE

I can hardly wait for tomorrow; it means a new life for me each and every day.

—STANLEY KUNITZ

Fall in love
with the energy
of the mornings

trace your fingers
along the lull
of the afternoons

take the spirit
of the evenings
in your arms
kiss it deeply

and then
make love
to the tranquility
of the nights.

—SANOBER KHAN

A healthy self-love
means we have
no compulsion to
justify to ourselves
or others why we
take vacations,
why we sleep late,
why we buy new shoes,
why we spoil ourselves
from time to time.

We feel comfortable
doing things which
add quality and
beauty to life.

—ANDREW MATTHEWS

Enjoy the peace
of Nature and
declutter your
inner world.

—AMIT RAY

DON'T HOLD
TO ANGER,
HURT, OR
PAIN. THEY
STEAL YOUR
ENERGY AND
KEEP YOU
FROM LOVE.

—LEO BUSCAGLIA

The only time
you fail is when
you fall down
and stay down.

—STEPHEN RICHARDS

LOOKING AT
BEAUTY IN
THE WORLD
IS THE FIRST
STEP OF
PURIFYING
THE MIND.

—AMIT RAY

We humans have lost the wisdom of genuinely resting and relaxing. We worry too much. We don't allow our bodies to heal, and we don't allow our minds and hearts to heal.

—THICH NHAT HANH

There is strange comfort in knowing that no matter what happens today, the sun will rise again tomorrow.

—AARON LAURITSEN

When sleep puts an
end to delirium, it is
a good symptom.

—HIPPOCRATES

There are nights when
the wolves are silent and
only the moon howls.

—GEORGE CARLIN

Those who
contemplate the
beauty of the earth
find reserves of
strength that will
endure as long
as life lasts.

—RACHEL CARSON

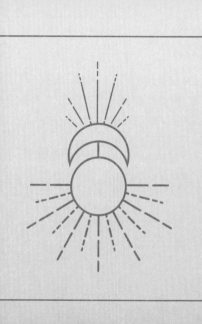

Knowing how to be solitary is central to the art of loving. When we can be alone, we can be with others without using them as a means of escape.

—BELL HOOKS

The past is a place
of reference, not a
place of residence;
the past is a place
of learning, not a
place of living.

—ROY T. BENNETT

Most of the things
we need to be most
fully alive never
come in busyness.
They grow in rest.

—MARK BUCHANAN

Nowhere can a man
find a quieter or
more untroubled
retreat than in
his own soul.

—MARCUS AURELIUS

NATURE IS
NOT A PLACE
TO VISIT.
IT IS HOME.

—GARY SNYDER

There is no problem on earth that can't be ameliorated by a hot bath and a cup of tea.

—JASPER FFORDE

We do not want
merely to see beauty…
We want to be
united with the
beauty we see, to
pass into it, to receive
it into ourselves,
to bathe in it, to
become part of it.

—C. S. LEWIS

HAPPINESS
IS A HOT
BATH ON
A SUNDAY
AFTERNOON.

—A. D. POSEY

A quiet mind
cureth all.

—ROBERT BURTON

When you recover
or discover
something that
nourishes your
soul and brings
joy, care enough
about yourself to
make room for
it in your life.

—JEAN SHINODA BOLEN

The resting place of the mind is the heart. The only place the mind will ever find peace is inside the silence of the heart.

—ELIZABETH GILBERT

One of the
symptoms of
an approaching
nervous breakdown
is the belief that
one's work is
terribly important.

—BERTRAND RUSSELL

THIS IS WHERE
IT ALL BEGINS.
EVERYTHING
STARTS HERE,
TODAY.

—DAVID NICHOLLS

It's very refreshing to go away and take a break, to clear your head, and just get into something else.

—FRANÇOIS NARS

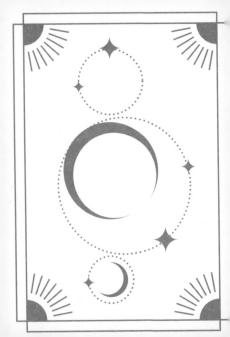

You cannot swim
for new horizons
until you have
courage to lose
sight of the shore.

—WILLIAM FAULKNER

JUST
BREATHING
CAN BE SUCH
A LUXURY
SOMETIMES.

—WALTER KIRN

When you press
the pause button on
a machine, it stops.
But when you
press the pause
button on human
beings, they start.

—DOV SEIDMAN

To rest was to
receive all aspects
of the world
without judgment.

—MICHAEL ONDAATJE

There comes a time
when the world gets
quiet, and the only
thing left is your own
heart. So you'd better
learn the sound of it.
Otherwise, you'll
never understand
what it's saying.

—SARAH DESSEN

Man can be himself only so long as he is alone; and if he does not love solitude, he will not love freedom; for it is only when he is alone that he is really free.

—ARTHUR SCHOPENHAUER

Each person
deserves a day
away in which
no problems
are confronted,
no solutions
searched for.

—MAYA ANGELOU

In this moment, there is plenty of time. In this moment, you are precisely as you should be. In this moment, there is infinite possibility.

—VICTORIA MORAN

The light music of
whiskey falling into
glasses made an
agreeable interlude.

—JAMES JOYCE

Don't mistake
activity with
achievement.

—JOHN WOODEN

Sometimes the most important thing in a whole day is the rest we take between two deep breaths.

—ETTY HILLESUM

KNOWLEDGE
SPEAKS,
BUT WISDOM
LISTENS.

—JIMI HENDRIX

We daydream to heal, to hope, to be happier. It is mental and emotional therapy. Daydreams are experiences both imagined and

felt, which makes
them very real to
the mind and the
heart. So relax.
Smile. Daydream.

—RICHELLE E.
GOODRICH

I have always been delighted at the prospect of a new day, a fresh try, one more start, with perhaps a bit of magic waiting somewhere behind the morning.

—J. B. PRIESTLEY

Sunshine is delicious,
rain is refreshing,
wind braces us up,
snow is exhilarating;
there is really no such
thing as bad weather,
only different kinds
of good weather.

—JOHN RUSKIN

Live in each season
as it passes;
breathe the air,
drink the drink,
taste the fruit,
and resign yourself
to the influence
of the earth.

—HENRY DAVID
THOREAU

It's more than
a bath; it's a
transformative
experience. You're
searching for
buoyancy in the
soul and spring
in your step.

—AMY LEIGH MERCREE

In times of stress,
the best thing we can
do for each other
is to listen with our
ears and our hearts,
and to be assured
that our questions
are just as important
as our answers.

—FRED ROGERS

Let the breath
lead the way.

—SHARON SALZBERG

All truly
great thoughts
are conceived
while walking.

—FRIEDRICH NIETZSCHE

Tomorrow is a new day. You shall begin it serenely and with too high a spirit to be encumbered with your old nonsense.

—RALPH WALDO EMERSON

In this game,
everyone needs
a break to refuel,
recharge, and jump
back in full throttle.

—HELEN EDWARDS

POETRY
HEALS THE
WOUNDS
INFLICTED
BY REASON.

—NOVALIS

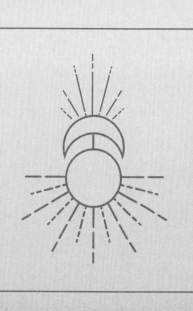

Accept where you are, accept what you have, accept who you are. Do what you can with all of that, and let it be enough.

—NIKKI ROWE

Our stresses,
anxieties, pains,
and problems
arise because we
do not see the
world, others, or
even ourselves as
worthy of love.

—PREM PRAKASH

ONE OF THE
BEST WAYS TO
RECHARGE
IS BY SIMPLY
BEING IN THE
PRESENCE
OF ART.

—DEAN FRANCIS ALFAR

You can only
lose something
that you have,
but you cannot
lose something
that you are.

—ECKHART TOLLE

Sleep's what we need. It produces an emptiness in us into which sooner or later energies flow.

—JOHN CAGE

If you suddenly and
unexpectedly feel
joy, don't hesitate.
Give in to it.

—MARY OLIVER

You attract and
manifest whatever
corresponds to
your inner state.

—ECKHART TOLLE

INSTEAD OF
WORRYING
ABOUT WHAT
YOU CANNOT
CONTROL,
SHIFT YOUR
ENERGY TO
WHAT YOU
CAN CREATE.

—ROY T. BENNETT

My friend... care for your psyche... know thyself, for once we know ourselves, we may learn how to care for ourselves.

—SOCRATES

People who do a creative job have to be alone to recharge their batteries. You can't live twenty-four hours a day in the spotlight and remain creative. For people like me, solitude is a victory.

—KARL LAGERFELD

Sometimes you need to sit lonely on the floor in a quiet room in order to hear your own voice and not let it drown in the noise of others.

—CHARLOTTE ERIKSSON

Whosoever
is delighted
in solitude is
either a wild
beast or a god.

—ARISTOTLE

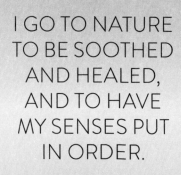

I GO TO NATURE
TO BE SOOTHED
AND HEALED,
AND TO HAVE
MY SENSES PUT
IN ORDER.

—JOHN BURROUGHS

We need time to defuse, to contemplate. Just as in sleep our brains relax and give us dreams, so at some time in the day we need to disconnect, reconnect, and look around us.

—LAURIE COLWIN

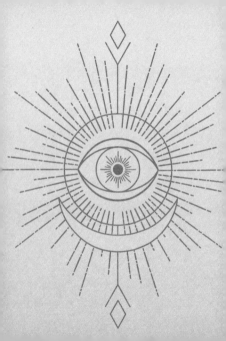

Everywhere I have
sought peace
and not found it,
except in a corner
with a book.

—THOMAS À KEMPIS

I don't think of all
the misery but of
the beauty that
still remains.

—ANNE FRANK

YOU ARE
WORTHY OF
EVERY DROP
OF SWEETNESS
AND EASE
THAT YOU
ENCOUNTER.

—ALEXANDRA ELLE

Self-care is never
a selfish act—it
is simply good
stewardship of
the only gift I
have, the gift I was
put on earth to
offer to others.

—PARKER PALMER

While some question whether Stillness is selfish, it's the opposite. It gives you greater capacity to embrace others… As the saying goes, you can't pour from an empty cup.

—DARCY LUOMA

Choose to be in touch with what is wonderful, refreshing, and healing within yourself and around you.

—THICH NHAT HANH

MANAGING
OUR STRESS
AND OUR REST
IS A SIGN OF
LIVING WISELY.

—SALLY CLARKSON

Meditation is a way
for nourishing and
blossoming the
divinity within you.

—AMIT RAY

As if you could
kill time without
injuring eternity.

—HENRY DAVID
THOREAU

Just when you feel you have no time to relax, know that this is the moment you most need to make time to relax.

—MATT HAIG

THE WISE
REST AT LEAST
AS HARD AS
THEY WORK.

—MOKOKOMA
MOKHONOANA

In this fast-paced world, it's important to slow down sometimes.

—DANO JANOWSKI

Nothing is more
important than
reconnecting with
your bliss.
Nothing is as rich.
Nothing is more real.

—DEEPAK CHOPRA

Mindfulness
is contrary to
mindlessness, yet
both fit quite well
in the spectrum of
ways to recharge
the human brain.

—MEHNAZ ANSARI

The goal of life
is to make your
heartbeat match
the beat of the
universe, to match
your nature
with Nature.

—JOSEPH CAMPBELL

Relax and refuse to let worry and stress rule your life. There is always a solution to every problem. Things will work out for you when you take time to relax, refresh, restore, and recharge your soul.

—LAILAH GIFTY AKITA

Rest until you
feel like playing,
then play until you
feel like resting,
period. Never do
anything else.

—MARTHA BECK

For a spirit that roamed restlessly, entering into every jot of the teeming life around him, stillness must have held a deep allure. If you are everything and everywhere, how restful it must seem to be no one and nowhere.

—MARK DOTY

You can do this,
and if you can't
do it today, you'll
do it tomorrow.
You are not a failure.

—ALISHA RAI

Try to pause
each day and
take a walk to
view nature.

—LAILAH GIFTY
AKITA

THE MOST WASTED OF ALL DAYS IS ONE WITHOUT LAUGHTER.

—NICOLAS CHAMFORT

You are
never alone.
You are eternally
connected
with everyone.

—AMIT RAY

Reading is a respite from the restlessness of technology, but it's not only that. It's how I reset and recharge. It's how I escape, but it's also how I engage. And reading should spur further engagement.

—WILL SCHWALBE

To sit in the shade on a fine day and look upon verdure is the most perfect refreshment.

—JANE AUSTEN

It is necessary to take breaks, set parameters, and be kind to yourself if you want to continue making an impact in your little corner of the world.

—CYNTHIA MENDENHALL

Do not ruin
today with
mourning
tomorrow.

—CATHERYNNE
M. VALENTE

Self-care is
how you take
your power back.

—LALAH DELIA

How beautiful it
is to do nothing,
and then to
rest afterward.

—SPANISH PROVERB

Sometimes we spend so much time and energy thinking about where we want to go that we don't notice where we happen to be.

—DAN GUTMAN

The most valuable
thing we can do for the
psyche, occasionally,
is to let it rest, wander,
live in the changing
light of a room,
not try to be or do
anything whatever.

—MARY SARTON

"What happens
when people open
their hearts?"

"They get better."

—HARUKI MURAKAMI

Just like there's always time for pain, there's always time for healing.

—JENNIFER BROWN

REST IS NOT IDLENESS.

—JOHN LUBBOCK

There is such freedom in being able to celebrate and appreciate the unique moments that recharge you and give you peace and joy.

—JENNY LAWSON

To understand the
immeasurable,
the mind must
be extraordinarily
quiet, still.

—JIDDU KRISHNAMURTI

THE ENERGY OF THE MIND IS THE ESSENCE OF LIFE.

—ARISTOTLE

Activity and rest are two vital aspects of life. To find a balance in them is a skill in itself. Wisdom is knowing when to have rest, when to have activity, and how much of each to have.

—SRI SRI RAVI SHANKAR

Nothing is worth diminishing your health. Nothing is worth poisoning yourself into stress, anxiety, and fear.

—STEVEN MARABOLI

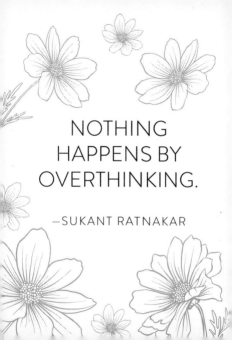

NOTHING HAPPENS BY OVERTHINKING.

—SUKANT RATNAKAR

Good friends, good books, and a sleepy conscience: this is the ideal life.

—MARK TWAIN

Reflect upon your present blessings— of which every man has many— not on your past misfortunes, of which all men have some.

—CHARLES DICKENS

Vulnerability
is the birthplace of
innovation, creativity,
and change.

—BRENÉ BROWN

Yesterday I was clever, so I wanted to change the world. Today I am wise, so I am changing myself.

—RUMI

Mandala Publishing
P.O. Box 3088
San Rafael, CA 94912
www.mandalaearth.com

Find us on Facebook: www.facebook.com/MandalaEarth
Follow us on Twitter: @MandalaEarth
Follow us on Instagram: @MandalaEarth

CEO: Raoul Goff
Editorial Director: Katie Killebrew
VP Creative: Chrissy Kwasnik
VP Manufacturing: Alix Nicholaeff
Associate Art Director: Ashley Quackenbush
Designers: Amy DeGrote and Lola Villanueva
Project Editor: Claire Yee
Editorial Assistant: Sophia R Wright
Production Associate: Andy Harper

ISBN: 978-1-64722-642-8
Manufactured in China by Insight Editions
10 9 8 7 6 5 4 3 2 1
2022 2023 2024

Also available:
Recharge: A Day and Night Reflection Journal
ISBN: 978-1-64722-208-6